# CASE MANAGER
## Coloring book



THIS COLORING BOOK
BELONGS TO:

Instant
CASE
MANAGER
Just Add
COFFEE

DON'T MAKE
ME USE MY
CASE MANAGER
Voice

WORLD'S
Okayest
CASE
MANAGER

THIS DAY IS SUCH AS A
CLUSTERF*CK
AND
I DON'T GIVE A
SHIT!

THIS
CASE
MANAGER
IS OFF
DUTY

STFU!
JUST ASSUME
I'M
Always
RIGHT!

case manager
llama
ain't got time
for your
drama

A FUCKING
LEGEND

CASE MANAGER
BECAUSE BADASS
MIRACLE WORKER
ISN'T AN OFFICIAL
JOB TITLE

i miss
your
stupid
face

OF COURSE
I TALK TO
MYSELF.
SOMETIMES
I NEED
EXPERT
ADVICE.

WHAT
THE
ACTUAL
FUCK?

CAUTION!
CASE
MANAGER
AT
WORK

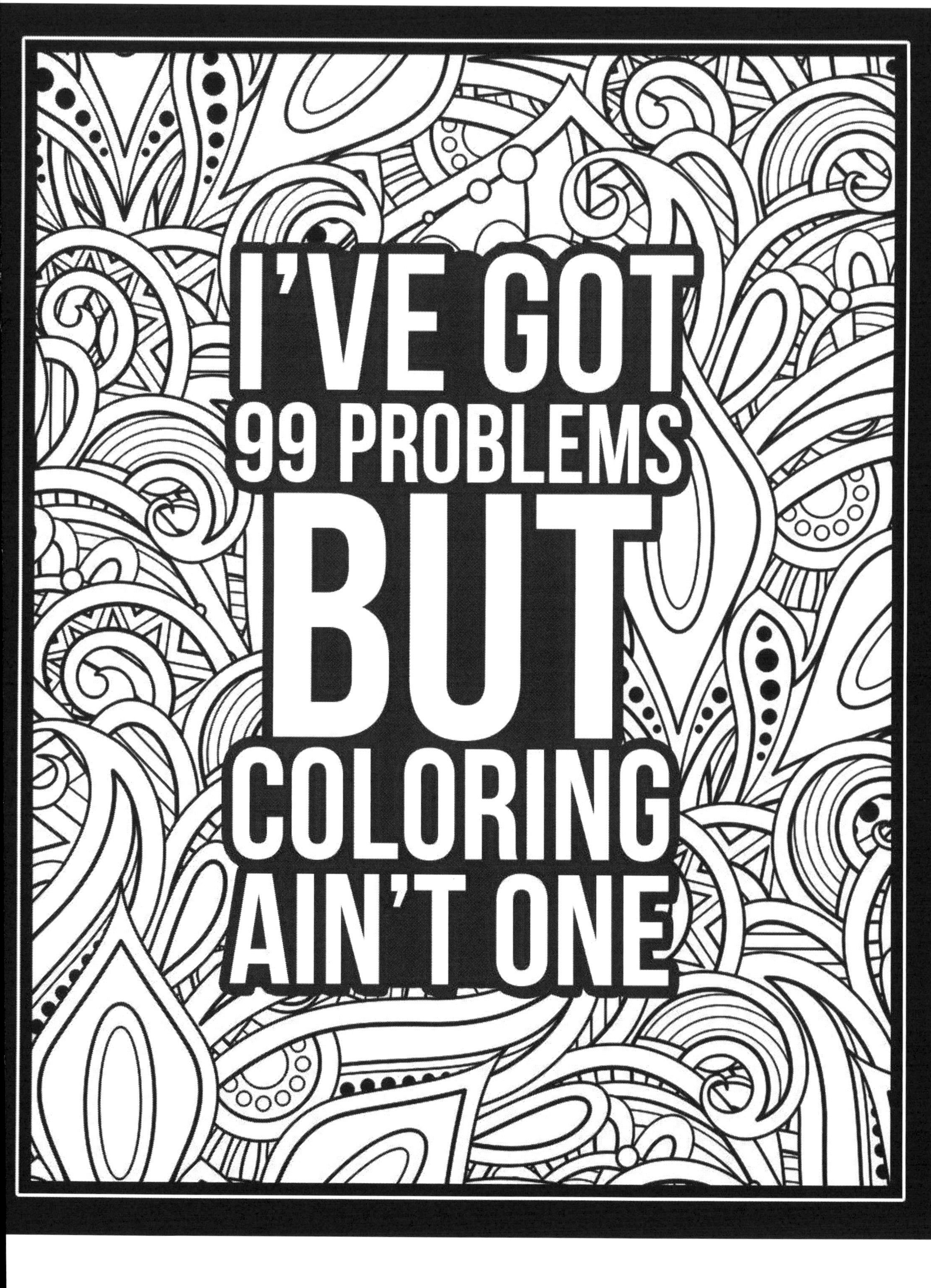
I'VE GOT
99 PROBLEMS
BUT
COLORING
AIN'T ONE

I'm a
Case Manager
What's your
Super
Power?

Shit
HAPPENS

IT'S A
CASE
MANAGER
THING
YOU'D NOT
UNDERSTAND

THIS
CASE
MANAGER
NEEDS A MOTHER
FUCKING DRINK

Essential
AF

SORRY
I AM DONE
HELPING
ASSHOLES
TODAY

Made in the USA
Las Vegas, NV
30 September 2022

56233368R00026